THIN AIR

THIN AIR

JOHN MOLE

Shoestring Press

Printed by imprintdigital
Upton Pyne, Exeter
www.digital.imprint.co.uk

Typesetting and cover design by The Book Typesetters
us@thebooktypesetters.com
07422 598 168
www.thebooktypesetters.com

Published by Shoestring Press
19 Devonshire Avenue, Beeston, Nottingham, NG9 1BS
(0115) 925 1827
www.shoestringpress.co.uk

First published 2021
© Copyright: John Mole
© Copyright author photograph: Benjamin Mole

The moral right of the author has been asserted.

ISBN 978-1-912524-94-5

This group of poems accumulated throughout periods of lockdown necessitated by the virus Covid-19 between late March 2020 and February 2021. It is in every sense occasional and anecdotal, consisting of observations, meditations, reminiscences and anticipations. Some poems seek to give voice to personal and social anxieties, others to find consolatory humour and delight in the unexpected. Many have been posted on Instagram and as contributions to the online *Plague20journal,* a record of the period by different voices in different places (Plague20journal.com).

CONTENTS

DISTANCING

I walk alone
in familiar company

stepping aside
abruptly from myself,

from who I was
to who I am,

our distance kept
for health and safety's sake.

A long gaze meets
in the space between us,

becomes the ghost
of pale necessity

but promises
a swift reunion

when we walk together
as we surely shall.

OUT WALKING

If you see me coming
better step aside.

A lot of men didn't
and a lot of men died . . .

Out walking now
I remember this song

as I measure my distance
not to avoid death

but to help save lives.
See me perfect my neighbourly

swerve and dip
away from the pavement

or my deft parabola
when exercising in the park,

part virtue, part apology,
and always with a smile.

FIERCE BEAUTY

Curious or indifferent,
either way

the natural world
surrounds us

blind though we've often been
to such fierce beauty.

As Blake saw heaven
in one wild flower

so now let us celebrate
the earth's abundance

and its generative
consolation,

root and branch
becoming blossom

loosened on the air
in purer light.

DAILINESS

Humming an old tune
under your breath

as you saunter
down an empty street.

This is the routine
of dailiness,

swinging each arm
to keep the other company.

A practised nonchalance,
the occasional deft

skip in your step
like Fred Astaire

or, hands behind your back,
you stop to take a bow

as if the sound of silence
were applause.

SILENCE

Silence is welcome
when the talking stops

and second thoughts
get lost in meditation

as the mind sets out
to rediscover certainty

with patient steps
across familiar ground.

It measures every word
along the way

and is reassured
by cautious speech

which hesitates
before returning

in a fresh configuration
as the silence breaks.

COMFY

Moonglow, Star Dust,
Honeysuckle Rose,

Lullaby of Birdland
and The Man I Love.

As Auden found with lakes
I've found with songs

that 'just reeling off their names
is ever so comfy.'

Sustained in these times
by melody at random

I'm grateful when a title
summons it to mind

so Fly Me to the Moon,
Come on Get Happy,

My Funny Valentine,
It Had to be You.

EN ROUTE

Time has entered
the inside lane,

its rear-view mirror
a cracked glass.

Moving ahead
at a steady pace

it trusts in our patience
as we follow on.

Whether we share
a common destination

or are planning to take
a different route

becomes one and the same
when it turns around

to steal a quick glance
over its shoulder.

HOW

How you wake
to yesterday's dreaming,

how one day
dissolves in the next,

how companionship
keeps pace with caution,

how memory
waits for its chance,

how tomorrow
might be the question,

how silence
considers it best,

how you turn
to the absence behind you,

how the answer
is what lies ahead.

AHEAD

The way ahead
is fraught with purpose

searching for itself
to lighten up,

to lose the weight
of retrospective milestones

burdened by regret
and chances missed.

What may be reached
remains uncertain,

hopeful horizons
partially in view,

the tentative release
of one step nearer

in a direction
found by starting out.

NEVER

Never to confuse
movement with action

was Hemingway's advice
to Marlene Dietrich.

In isolation
I have remembered this

so plan the day
accordingly.

A little now
must go the distance

concentratedly
about its business,

not in miles
but in application,

never far from home
and holding fast.

THE JOURNEY

Speak on, old friend,
let me hear your voice

as we travel together
down the line.

This has become
an unexpected journey

but let the destination
not be silence.

When we arrive
may fellowship embrace us

as we step out
in its precious light

and once again
meet face to face

continuing the journey
through a brave new world.

SOME SUNNY DAY

Bunting and flags
on porch and doorstep,

cautious celebration
gathering in the street.

An elderly neighbour
singing from her garden

*We'll meet again
some sunny day.*

In the meantime
soldier on together,

prepare for a safe
and happy landing

just as the promise
of that sentimental song

still lifts the spirit
for an hour or two.

OUT OF NOWHERE

Scuffing up flint
along the old ways

in our boots or trainers
we'd rediscovered walking

as the paradox
of solitude for company

when out of nowhere
cyclists came crunching past

and thanked us
as we stepped aside.

Such unfamiliar courtesy
was so surprising

that we shouted after them
You're welcome! as they disappeared.

If this becomes the new way
may it last for ever.

TRUTH

If truth could be told
it would find in us

the single image
of itself alone.

No sideways glance,
no tentative evasion

but face to face
with what has passed.

It would wait patiently
while we sleep

in tangled thickets
of confusion

then step out
to guide our future

lit from within
by selfless love.

THE TREES

Departing summer
settles on their branches,

sings to the leaves
its lullaby of bronze

then vanishes
one autumn morning

as if summoned
overnight.

So they wake
in robes of russet,

a seasonal display
on winter's terms

and soon to be stripped
until next spring

to the skeletal limbs
of their nakedness.

THE TRICK

Early evening light
arrives on time

and brings a welcome
gift of closure.

The moon appears
to lift its lantern,

guiding us silently
toward the dawn.

Shadows gather
on our brickwork,

melancholy splendour
lies along the grass,

distraction plays around
with lines of poetry

hoping that words
may do the trick.

POSSIBILITIES

Here in this wood
small children race ahead,

their eagerness unleashed
from strict restraint.

Beneath an overhanging
latticework

they search out
pools of dappled light.

While keeping to the path
with all its possibilities

and improvising
like a line of verse

they surprise themselves
no less than us

who walk behind them
at a steadier pace.

WATER UNDER THE BRIDGE

Wherever it flows
is away from here,

carrying the moment
to become another

and leave you standing
while pale clouds gather

then reveal the sun
as a parting gift.

To come and to go
in whatever direction,

catching the light
that plays on its surface

and hinting at depths
that travel beneath

is a river's true course
and a poem's too.

THE STADIUM

Not even the sound
of one hand clapping

from empty seats
that need each other.

The absent teams
are hungry for applause

and the pitch
is green with envy.

Accustomed to a roaring
tribal multitude

the stadium awaits
its gradual return,

for players to fill
this wilderness of silence

with thundering boots
and welcome heavy breath.

OUR GHOSTS

They have a way with them,
so quiet as they arrive

yet hauntingly convivial
and glad to be together.

We welcome them
to family occasions,

grateful for their blessing
on companionable delight.

This must be the day
they join us to remember

every happiness
that once they shared

and to join the memory
our future has in store

before they leave
as quietly as they came.

QUESTIONS

Asked too many questions
at the dinner table

like what was next
or could we have cake for afters,

my mother's answers
always came out the same —

pudding was Wait and See
or Finish What's on your Plate.

I thought of her today
when someone asked me

just how long I thought
this isolation would go on

as if it were a meal
that seemed to last forever

and we were restless children
asking to get down.

ADMONITIONS

So you've made your bed
now lie on it.

For goodness' sake
stop pulling that face.

If the wind changes
you'll be stuck with it.

Don't care
was made to care.

I tell myself
all this and more,

recalling childhood's
sternest admonitions

as I wander ghostly
round the house and garden,

spirited away
from then to now.

CIRCUMSTANCE

Take your ease now
and be grateful for it.

So says Circumstance,
holding the key.

Doors open again
on nervous hinges,

faces are released
from isolation's grip

with bright eyes smiling
above their masks

and muffled laughter
tentatively shared

while Circumstance still
sounds its note of warning

Don't get too excited
as if speaking to a child

but thank you for your patience.
Have a good day.

AS IF

Looking at his watch
to see what time it is

as if time itself were stealing
the minutes from the hours,

looking at the calendar's
reciprocal blank gaze

as if somehow tomorrow
might be different from today,

looking intently at himself
though only half-awake

as if a puzzled stranger
had risen from his bed,

considering life's vague options
and planning what to do

as if they might come suddenly
to offer him a choice.

BUBBLES

1945/2020

Sitting in the garden
with a little clay pipe

and a ready basin
at my feet

I was that Child's World
painting by Millais

as I blew soapy bubbles
to catch the light.

I think of them now
as a strange transparency,

each one with a face
that presses to be seen

while it floats off to join
whatever couple

in the bubble permitted
by decree.

CONTACTLESS

Pay by card if possible
instead of with cash

and make it contactless
to keep things simple.

Face to face
says not to set foot

across the ubiquitous
yellow line.

Accept that acquaintance
is a casual elbow bump

and social distancing
an oxymoron.

Absence of contact
plans to keep us safe

but weighs its authority
against our loss.

ELBOWS

Old Possum
on the dance floor

late in life
was known to friends as

Elbows Eliot
who partnered Valerie

with awkward
angular affection.

No doubt there were
occasions for apology

but both of them
might now be shocked

to find that what was once
the bump to be avoided

would become the safest way
to greet a friend.

ALL LIFE

Laughter was always
breaking out

but sorrow
kept its counsel.

Memory came always
in two minds,

but then chose one
according to the weather.

Hope was always
ready to arrive

but never without
a note of caution.

Love remained
and held its breath

as if all life
depended on it.

TAKE A BREATH

and hold it tight
in expectation

as a thoughtful pause
anticipates release.

When you're ready
let it go

to travel innocently
through the air.

May it seek out
the sound of laughter

or your music played
to open ears.

May spontaneity
remain a virtue

and your next breath
be its own reward.

ALONG

Along with the smile
comes the raised eyebrow

that isn't quite sure
of what has been said.

Along with the promise
comes the proviso

that circumstance
may conspire to break it.

Along with today
come plans for tomorrow

that may change by the hour
or at the last minute.

Along with each nuance
comes yet another

that admits hesitation
and hangs in the air.

NUANCE

Considering the balance
between this and that

let thinking be readiness
to change its mind

in generous argument
admitting nuance

and never call this
sitting on the fence.

Let truth lie
in shades of meaning

carried into light
and recognised as such

then face to face
in firm agreement

welcome decisiveness
by shaking hands.

BRIEFING

Haunted eyes
above a podium

belie the reassurance
of authority.

Nervous glances
at the telescreen

anticipate bewilderment's
interrogation.

Mutual uncertainties
preside and hesitate,

confront each other
face to face

keeping their distance
as the rules require

before they leave the virus
to an empty room.

GRANULAR

Crumbs of slight comfort
fall from the newsdesk

as piecemeal statisics
to keep us informed

or as grains, seeds,
each planted in hope

that tomorrow's harvest
will not fail.

Thus another word
takes on a new meaning

to join the many
that this year has endorsed;

precision as metaphor
printed in numbers,

a granular lexicon
not lost for words.

CENTRE STAGE

This is the theatre
of waking dreams

become a nightmare
played out scene by scene.

Wisdom and Patience
huddle in the wings

as Fear has taken
centre stage.

He struts and frets
with viral gestures

in expectation
of applause

while empty seats
refuse to grant it,

calling for the curtain
to come down.

OUR DIRECTOR

This movie we're in
is running over budget

and our director
has problems with the script.

We have been hired
as furloughed extras,

keeping a measured
distance from each other

which just won't work
in spontaneous crowd scenes

or a planned gathering
for family events.

So our director
from his lonely canvas seat

tries to explain to us
what may come next.

UNMASKED

Liberated faces
break into a smile

although they still wear
that distant look;

such freedom
not yet to be trusted,

such promise
yet to be fulfilled.

A furrowed brow
extends each lifeline

searching out
its lost horizon

while beyond
the present moment

ambiguous future
grins from ear to ear.

THE KEY

Open up, walk out
and throw away your key.

How eager it is
to leave the sullen lock.

Watch as it disappears
through a residual dark

that brightens even now
to speed its welcome flight.

Trace where it lands
among the gradual changes,

the many open doors,
the groups, the gatherings

then let it lie there
beyond reclamation,

gratefully disowned
and yet still yours.

CONVERSATION

Loneliness, greeting
its other self,

is never at a loss
for conversation,

loss being
what they have in common,

the anecdotal
bond between them.

Time and again
they turn to one another,

prompted by memory
and desire;

what almost was,
what might have been

if only life
had found the words.

SLOW LIGHT

Slow light illuminates
the waking street

as windows exchange
their daily messages.

An open door
anticipates arrival

and a welcome mat
is duly laid.

Let now be the time
for cautious promises,

for hope to listen
with half-open ear

as tongue-tied custom
once more finds a voice

and rediscovers
what it feared was lost

MEASURES

Neither the progress
of a melody

harmonious accumulation
bar by bar

nor the reckoning
of distance to be travelled

with various options
open for return

but the unwelcome
bullet points of paperwork

becoming policy
restrictively laid down

perhaps with luck
to prove provisional

and gradually removed
if circumstance allows.

THE CIRCUIT

Such a scattering
of lost connections,

their fragile circuit
already broken

as the loose ends
search for one another,

hoping for light
and reconciliation.

May opportunity
hold out a hand

to reach the tangle
of impatience,

finding its disconnections
one by one

and mending the circuit
for us all.

GREEN SHOOTS

Taking fresh aim
at yet another year

they keep it closely
in their sights

at first uncertain,
nervous of the trigger,

then firing promises
they plan to keep.

Invisible at first
they wait in hiding,

ubiquitous metaphors
for imminent surprise,

undercover conscripts
gathering as an army

to march on Summer
with their glorious display.

EVERYBODY OUT

is not the shrill command
of a union leader

but the persuasion
of this morning's sun.

Runners pass by
in their sheathes of lycra

and a cyclist's helmet
catches the light.

A brightness glows
in the chatter of children

and dogs out walking
tug at their leads

while the park is already
a field full of folk

as that line from Langland
shines where they meet.

LIGHT YEARS

They come to mind
so distant now

and take our memory
by surprise.

Casting no shadow
their sudden brilliance

is love's return
in its own good time.

Released at last
from an anxious burden,

the weight of darkness
and dismay,

they shine for us
on troubled waters

yet keep their distance
as we wake.

REACHING FOR LIGHT

This was not a sleep
to be willingly continued

as your waking from it
in the early hours

offered a hesitant
ambiguous release

into a strangeness
more familiar.

Reaching for light
you wondered

if what had seemed a dream
was mere bewilderment,

a haunted narrative
of apprehension,

or just residual darkness
welcoming you back.

THRESHOLD

Exchanging one horizon
for another

as we cross the threshold
of anticipation

we gaze in both directions,
balancing loss and gain

in equal measure
while we move ahead.

Bewilderment and gratitude
direct our looking back

to where the thin air
that so much has vanished into

first surprised us
with its welcome strangeness

promising then as now
a trust to be restored.